Hell Beneath My Feet

Hell Beneath My Feet

Sandra Mayfield

Sandra Mayfield Publishing

Sandra Mayfield Publishing LLC
957 Coburn rd
Clarksville Tn 37042
www.Sandramayfieldpublishing.com
phone: 931-249-5338

Published by Sandra Mayfield Publishing 09/20/2023

ISBN:979-8-218-96507-5

Content

LORD

Lord Walk with me
lord carry me
lord help me to understand the wrong I have done
lord keep me safe
Lord keep me whole
lord keep me humble
keep me in your sights
keep me and never let me let myself down
lord it would not be me without you
lord I am your disciple

Lord

MY BEAUTIFUL FLOWER

You came ot us
Like a wind ready to mow down
Anyone who got in your way
of you getting to that
special someone in your heart
you loved him unconditionally
and that special someone is Yakub
you made sure rthat he was
well taken care of
you gave heim a love that anyone would love to have
and now you are with a love
who will hold you in his arms and
carry you to the light of heaven

My beautiful Flower

EYES OF THE HOURGLASS

The soul of the person is an hourglass
called our eyes
one that is full of
sorrow
hate
love
happiness
sadness
But look real close to see which one is there
before you say I do

Eyes of the hourglass

MY YOUTH

Where are our kids today
won't play Honey honey bee bop
hopscotch
redlight greenlight
stop
the violence
you are only hurting
your generation
your kids
your Mother
your sisters
your brothers why you figure
you can take a life
without any
remorse
or heart break
you are only killing
and the next little one of your self
more heart aches
why do you think they are building more jails
for you my children
your black skin
why keep letting them win

My Youth

PITY

I will give you my heart
I will give you my hands and legs
and every ounce of me
but what I won't give you is pity

Pity

WHERE ARE YOU

Where are you
when I am sad
when I need you
I am always there for you
I have curried you when you were down
where are you when I need love
understanding
to be held
to put a smile on my face
where are you when I need a voice
to say I love you
unconditionally

Where are you

MY BACK

You said you had my back
We were trained to watch each others back
so like brothers and sisters
in silence we watch each others back
I never see you there
but I know you are

My Back

I KNOW YOU

I know you
but you don't know me
I can't believe the dream I see
because the dream
doesn't belong to me
I see where you are going
I see where you have been
and now I understand
the message you sent
not all is equal
not all is fair
and when times get hard
we must prepair
not for hardship and not for pain
but when we are one big family again

I know you

FAMILY

FAMILY

What is a family
one who supposed to love you
unconditionally
to have when times are hard
for laughter
for guidence
sometime to fight with
just have someone around to cry
with you when times are hard
you dont have to be blood to be
family

Family

BETRAYED

you have betrayed me in so many ways
how do I began
1 lie
2 hurt
3 not who you say you are
4 trust
5 evil
6 egotistic
7 dog women
8 womanizer
and most of all
My love for you

Betrayed

ANGER

I am so angry until I can burst
I am trying to hold on
everytime I look at him I get mader and mader
how can I get myself under control
when everytime he keeps doing the same thing over
and over again
same thing different day

Anger

Pain

Part I

I come to you with pain
you cut me open
just to cause me more pain
I come back to you again for your help
once again you keep me in pain
you sent for test
but because of politice
I am not getting the care I need
so I am still in pain
so tell me
what am I supposed to do
when everyone keep on saying
the insurance only let
you do so much
no matter how much you pay each month
to supposed to get the treatment you neeed
so I won't have to go through this pain
so for all of you
with health insurance
at the end of the bill
you still in pain

Pain

MARY

how sweet sure a beautiful
person helping out raising all of us
always made sure that
we made it to school on time
there is no one
like our sister Mary
we love you more than life itself
we would never give up on you
and we know
you will never stop fighting
to come home
to kick our bottoms
like you used too

Mary

THE SPILL OF BLOOD

we are americans
I hear you coming
your lights are so bright
your sirens blasting so loud
But I wonder are you here for me
to help or to hurt
our blood runs the same
but when you change into another uniform
beleive you are better than us
because you have on a different uniform
so tell me Mr policeman
who are you our savior or our killer

The spill of blood

JEALOUSY WHY

Because your skin is lighter
because you look better
because you have more than I
because you are in a nice ride
because you are in a nice house
so why are you so jealousy
of one another
we all come from the same place

think about it

Jealousy why

LOVE AND TRUST

one day you will have love
what is love supposed to be
caring
unconditional trust
foregiveness
honour yourself
hope
no one else but you in my heart
respect
that's what I am waiting for

Love and trust

www.ingramcontent.com/pod-product-compliance
Lightning Source LLC
Chambersburg PA
CBHW060200070426
42447CB00033B/2236